Understanding the Root, the Causes and the Remedy of the Middle East Conflict

Apostle Aaron B. Claxton

Understanding the Root, the Causes and the Remedy of the Middle East Conflict

Copyright © 2015 by Apostle Aaron B. Claxton

All rights reserved. No part of this book may be reproduced or transmitted in any form or by any means without written permission of the author.

ISBN Number: 978-0-9824550-8-1

Dedication

It gives me great pleasure to dedicate this book to my beloved and indispensable wife, of nearly 57 years.

She is not only my lover, confidante, but my helper, critic and encourager in everything I do including this book.

She is forever my typist, proofreader, advisor and all that I have ever needed in this business book writing.

Dr. Deborah J. Claxton has earned several degrees and has of late received her doctorate of Religious Education- and is an author in her own right.

Thank God for "Dr. Deborah," as she is affectionately known by many, and "Sugar Lump," as she is known by me.

Acknowledgements

I would like to acknowledge my secretary, Elder Theresa Ward, as a very faithful, untiring worker who always finishes her assignments ahead of time.

Elder Theresa Ward has done the lion's share of typing and retyping the manuscript of this book.

May the Lord ever bless her for her steadfastness and dependability.

Table of Contents

Dedication i

Acknowledgements ii

Chapter 1 - *Biblical and Spiritual Roots of the Mideast Conflict* . 1

Chapter 2 - *Historical and Ethnic Causes of the Mideast Conflict* 5

Chapter 3 - *Geographical Roots and Biblical Authenticity* 11

Chapter 4 - *Historical Realities* 21

Chapter 5 - *Muslims Resent Those Who Help Israel* 29

Chapter 6 - *Israel's Claims Documented* 31

Chapter 7 - *Insights into Islam's Deceptive Claims on the Holy Land* 43

Chapter 8 - *The Church and Others against the Jews* 53

Chapter 9 - *Here's God's Remedy for the Age Old Conflict* 61

Conclusion 67

About the Author 69

Chapter 1

Biblical and Spiritual Roots of the Mideast Conflict

I am a man past eighty years of age. I have been privileged to see many things come and go. But as long as I can remember, there has been some kind of striving over land rights in what we call the "Holy Land." It is said that this strip of land is about the size of the state of New Jersey.

Some call this land "Palestine" and others call it "Israel." Why has there been continuous fighting over this strip of land, especially since Israel was declared a <u>legal state</u> in 1948, by the United Nations?

Well, as our caption above suggests, this conflict in the Middle East has <u>biblical</u> and <u>spiritual roots</u>. This "Promised Land" that was deeded to Abraham and his offspring by Jehovah through a covenant, by way of Isaac and Jacob, was much larger in size than the two groups are fighting over today.

Understanding the Root, the Causes and the Remedy of the Middle East Conflict

When Jehovah God made an Everlasting Covenant with Abraham around 2000 B.C., as recorded in Genesis 15:15-21, he deeded all the land from the River of Egypt (the Nile?) to the River of Euphrates <u>forever</u> to Abraham and his Israeli seed. That is, all the land from around Lebanon to Iraq! This was far more than the little sliver of land that Israel now occupies.

The family drama concerning this land began to unfold in Genesis chapter sixteen, when Sarai, Abram's wife who was barren, gave her Egyptian handmaid, Hagar, to Abram to cohabit with, and she became pregnant by him, and bore Abram his firstborn son, Ishmael. Prior to the boy's birth, tensions arose between the two women and Hagar ran away, only to be met by the Angel of Jehovah who promised to make Ishmael a great and multitudinous nation, and sent her back to her mistress, Sarai.

In chapter seventeen of Genesis, the Lord appeared to Abram announcing Himself as <u>El Shaddai or God Almighty</u>. The Lord had not spoken to him for thirteen years. At this point, when Abram was ninety nine years old, the Lord told him to walk blamelessly before Him and He would complete or establish His Covenant with him. He commanded Abraham to be circumcised and to circumcise all the males in his household in their foreskins, as a <u>sign</u> of the Covenant. Ishmael was included in the circumcising.

The Lord changed Abram's name to <u>Abraham</u> (father of many nations) and He changed Sarai's name to <u>Sarah</u> meaning <u>princess</u>. The time for them to receive their long awaited, promised son had finally arrived, after more than twenty five years of waiting! He was ninety nine and she was eighty nine years old. Their miraculously born son, <u>Isaac</u> would be born the very next year, when they would be 100 and 90 years old respectively.

It is in this chapter (Genesis Chapter 17) that the drama heightens. The aforementioned covenant between Abraham and El Shaddai involved Abraham and his descendants <u>through Isaac</u>, and those <u>descendants</u> were to receive as a <u>possession</u> or <u>inheritance</u>, "All the land of Canaan, (from Lebanon to Iraq) as an <u>everlasting possession</u>, and 'I (Jehovah) will be their God'" (not Allah!) (Gen. 17:8).

Chapter 2

Historical and Ethnic Causes of the Mideast Conflict

It is in this same chapter (chapter seventeen of the book of Genesis) after Abraham was told by Jehovah (El Shaddai), "I will establish My Covenant <u>with him</u> (Isaac) for <u>an everlasting Covenant</u> and with <u>his</u> descendants after him." Abraham protested saying, "Oh that Ishmael might live before you!" Then God said, "<u>NO!</u>"

Here is where the issue of <u>inheritance rights</u> and the <u>rights of the firstborn</u> enter the picture. Let's turn to Genesis chapter 21 and listen in on the conversation. After Isaac was born and weaned (at around two years old) and during the weaning celebration, Sarah saw Hagar's son, Ishmael, scoffing at or making fun of her and her son, Isaac. "Therefore she said to Abraham, 'Cast out this <u>bondwoman and her son</u>; for the son of this bondwoman <u>shall not be heir with my son</u>...'

"And the matter was very displeasing in Abraham's sight because of his son (Ishmael). But God said to Abraham; 'Do not let it be displeasing in your sight because of the lad or because of your bondwoman. Whatever Sarah has said to you, listen to her voice. <u>For in Isaac your seed shall be called</u>. Yet, I <u>will also make a nation of the son of the bondwoman, because he is your seed</u>'" (Gen. 21:10-13).

Let's review and recap this picture as we consider the scriptural and historical roots of the present day Middle East Conflict. This conflict begins with Jehovah God assigning all the land of Canaan (from Lebanon to Iraq) to Abraham and his descendants through the line of Isaac and Jacob. Evidently the customs of the people of that time and place dictated that the <u>firstborn</u> son was entitled to the lion's share of the father's estate and assets at the time of his death.

Obviously, in Hagar's mind and Abraham's mind <u>Ishmael</u> was Abraham's "<u>firstborn son</u>" and therefore was entitled to inherit the best and the most of his father's possessions. God and Sarah made it clear in our scriptural references that <u>Isaac</u> was the son of choice and therefore <u>God's chosen heir</u> of God's Covenant and choicest blessings.

Listen further to the words of Eliezer, Abraham's oldest and highest ranked servant in his household: "The Lord has blessed my master greatly, and he has become great; and he has given him flocks and herds, silver and gold, male and female servants, and camels and donkeys. And Sarah my master's wife bore a son to my master when she was old; <u>and to him (Isaac) he has given all that he has</u>." (Gen. 24:35-36). And near the time of Abraham's death, it is written: "And <u>Abraham gave all that he had to Isaac</u>" (Gen 25:5).

All of Abraham's sons by Hagar, Sarah, and Keturah, Abraham's wife after Sarah died, were present at Abraham's burial. Through Keturah, Abraham produced six sons, and more Arabs. She was a black woman, and Moses took his wife from the tribe of <u>Midian</u>, one of Abraham's sons by Keturah (See Exodus 2:15-21; Numbers 12:1).

As we look further into this narrative we will observe how the Lord himself guarded and directed the <u>birthright</u> and <u>His blessing</u> upon Abraham's descendants through Isaac to assure that the Covenant blessings would pass down through God's chosen recipients, according to His <u>foreordained purposes</u>. The Apostle Paul recorded the following in one of his New Testament letters, "In Him (Christ Jesus) we also have obtained an inheritance, being predestined according to the purpose of Him (God the Father) who works all things according to the counsel of His (own) will" (Eph. 1:11, *Emphasis mine*).

Let's pick up on some rather strange and bizarre developments in this narrative of birthrights, blessings and the Covenant as they unfold in Genesis Chapters 25-28.

Here we find the story of Isaac's wife, Rebekah, when she was pregnant with twin boys. Rebekah found a struggle going on within her womb, and the Lord said to her: "Two nations are in your womb, two peoples shall be separated from your body; one people shall be stronger than the other and the older shall serve the younger, and the first came out red. He was like a hairy garment all over; so they called his name Esau (Hairy). Afterward his brother came out, and his hand took hold of Esau's heel, so his name was called Jacob (Heel catcher or Supplanter)" (Gen. 25: 23-26, NKJV).

As the narrative proceeds, we find that Jacob, the younger twin of Isaac and Rebekah on two occasions tricked his older brother Esau out of his firstborn birthright and his father Isaac's Covenant, spoken blessings.

Esau exclaimed, "Is he not rightly named Jacob? (Supplanter). For he has supplanted me these two times. He took away my blessing!" (Gen. 27:36).

Let's read further: "Esau saw that Isaac had blessed Jacob and sent him away to Padan Aram (Syria) to take himself a wife from there, and that as he blessed him, he gave him a charge saying, 'You shall not take a wife from the daughters of Canaan,' and that Jacob had obeyed his father and his mother and had gone to Padan Aram."

"Also Esau saw that the daughters of Canaan did not please Isaac, so Esau went to Ishmael and took Mahalah the daughter of Ishmael, Abraham's son (Esau's first cousin from the Egyptian side of the family) to be his wife, in addition to the two Hittite (Canaanite) wives he (already) had" (Gen. 28:6-9, *Emphasis mine*). Therefore Esau chose to identify with the Arabic side of Abraham's family.

Do you get the drift? God, through some strange moves orchestrated Jacob getting the birthright and the Covenant blessing (many offspring and the inheritance of the land of Canaan – the so called "Holy Land"). Esau, out of spitefulness toward his parents' wishes, married two Canaanite wives creating more Arabs, the first Arabs coming through the union of Abraham and Hagar. Then to add insult to injury, to spite his parents more, Esau proceeded to marry his <u>Arab cousin</u>, the daughter of Ishmael!

Is it any wonder that there are Christian scholars today who say that the so-called Palestinians are none other than the ancient <u>Edomites</u>, also known as the Esauites"?

This takes care of the ancient background of the present day Middle East conflict, between the combatants, the Israelis and the Arabs.

Chapter 3

Geographical Roots and Biblical Authenticity

From the time of Abraham, 2,000 B.C., to the time of Moses and Joshua, over 500 years have passed.

The book of Joshua, the successor of Moses, records how the children of Israel (Jacob) through three major military campaigns, involving more than thirty enemy armies, were able under Joshua's capable leadership, to vanquish all of the Canaanite oppossers; and they conquered the people and the land through Jehovah's invincible intervention.

Here were Joshua's marching orders from the Lord: "Now therefore, arise, <u>go over</u> this <u>Jordan (River)</u>, you and <u>all these people (several million)</u>, to <u>the land which I am giving to them (the children of Israel)</u>. Moses my servant is dead" *(Emphasis mine)*.

"Everyplace the sole of your foot will tread upon I have given you, as I said to Moses. From the wilderness <u>and this Lebanon</u> as far as the great river, the River Euphrates, <u>all the land of the Hittites</u>, and to the Great Sea (the Mediterranean Sea) toward the going down of the sun (toward the west), <u>shall be your territory</u>" (Josh. 1:2-4 *Emphasis mine*). Thus we have provided clear, biblical evidence that God gave the land to the Israelites.

DIVINE OWNERSHIP ROOTS

Interested observers might pose the question at this point, "Who is this 'Lord' who audaciously takes land from one group of people and hands it over to another group of people?" The answer to that question points to the major purpose of this book and can solve the age old question, "To whom does this 'Holy Land' really belong? We answer both questions by <u>identifying the Supreme Owner of the heavens and the earth</u>.

We find in the holy Bible an ethereal, angelic character named Melchizedek, a king/priest of Salem (the original site of Jerusalem), who served bread and wine to Abram. He is described as "the priest of God Most High (El-Elyon)," pronouncing the astounding blessing upon Abram, as follows: "Blessed be Abram of God Most High,

Possessor (Owner) of heaven and earth; and blessed be God Most High..." (Gen.14:18-20 *Emphasis mine*). The world does not accept Jehovah, the God of Abraham, Isaac and Jacob, who is also the God and Father of the Lord Jesus Christ, as the Sole Creator and Owner of the world!

The Jews do, and so do the Christians, who serve and worship the same God! If Jehovah is indeed the Creator and Owner of the universe – and He is – then the Holy Land is His to give to whomever He chooses! Jehovah did just that when He gave all the land of the Canaanites to Abraham and his seed (Christ) through the line of Isaac and Jacob!

The psalmist David, a major conqueror of the Holy Land at a later time, declared, "The earth is the Lord's and the fullness thereof, the world and they that dwell therein. For He founded it upon the seas, and established it upon the floods" (Ps. 24:1-2).

The world surely argues that this is the Judeo-Christian holy Book and its viewpoint! Well, what other faith has produced a book of predictive prophecy, covering hundreds of years using some 40 writers that has been fulfilled to the letter? Examine the religions of the world

– Buddhism, Taoism, Confucianism, Shintoism, Hinduism and Islam. <u>Not one</u> of these has produced <u>fulfilled predictive prophecy</u> like the Judeo/Christian faith and its holy book, the Bible!

Additionally, in my view, the highest and greatest of all Judeo/Christian prophecies fulfilled were the ones about the <u>birth</u> of Jesus the Messiah, the Savior of the world. Two of these messianic prophecies are found in the book of Isaiah. The one says, "Therefore the Lord Himself will give you a sign: 'Behold, <u>a virgin shall conceive and bear a son</u>, and shall call His name Immanuel (God with us)'" (Isa. 7:14)! And again, "For unto us a child is born, unto us a son is given…And His name will be called Wonderful, Counselor, Mighty God, Everlasting Father, Prince of Peace…"(Isa. 9:6, *Emphasis mine*).

Thirdly, there is the very pointed and <u>specific location</u> given of the Messiah, Jesus Christ's birth by the prophet Micah. Listen to his words: "But you, Bethlehem Ephratha (one of <u>several</u> *Bethlehems*) though you are little among the thousands of Judah; yet out of you shall come forth to Me (Jehovah God) The One to be Ruler in Israel (Christ the Lord) whose goings forth are from of old, from everlasting" (Micah 5:2, *Emphasis mine*). These prophecies were spoken some <u>eight hundred years before</u> Jesus

Christ was born! All true Christians know within their hearts that these prophecies are indeed true!

Let's take note of an interesting side note. Jehovah called Abram out of a country that practiced <u>idolatry</u>. One of the chief gods of Ur of the Chaldees was a <u>moon god called Sin</u>. I find it interesting that Muhammed, founder of the religion called Islam, chose one god out of their pantheon of gods (360 gods) Allah, who was <u>Arabia's moon god</u>! Jehovah called Abram out of idolatrous moon worship, and Muhammed led his followers into the worship of the <u>moon god, Allah</u>! The Lord rebuked and punished Israel for worshiping <u>celestial deities</u> such as the "queen of heaven" (Jer.7:18; 44:17-22). Islam is called an <u>astral</u> or celestial worshiping religion by theologians.

Before we move further, let's look at an open and dramatic demonstration of the fact and reality <u>of the identity of the one and only true and living God</u>. We find the record of this demonstration in I Kings 18 starting at verse 22, which says, "Then Elijah said to the people, 'I, I only, remain a prophet of the Lord, but Baal's prophets are 450 men.' Elijah had the false prophets to build their altar and prepare their animal sacrifice, and to put no fire under it. Elijah went on to say, 'Then you call on the name of your god, and I will call on the name of the Lord; <u>and the One Who answers by fire, let Him be God.</u>'

So they (the prophets of Baal) took the bullock which was given them and they dressed it, and called on the name of Baal (their Phoenician god), from morning even until noon, saying, 'O Baal, hear us, 'but there was no voice nor any that answered. And they leaped upon the altar that was made…And they cried aloud and cut themselves after their custom with knives and lances until the blood gushed out upon them.

Midday passed, and they played the part of prophets until the time for the offering of the evening sacrifice, but there was no voice, no answer, no one paid attention…

At the time of the offering of the evening sacrifice, Elijah the prophet came near and said, 'O Lord, the God of Abraham, Isaac, and Israel, let it be known this day that You are God in Israel and that I am Your servant and that I have done all these things at Your word (Elijah had soaked the altar and the sacrifice with copious quantities of water). Hear me, O Lord, hear me that this people may know you, the Lord (Jehovah), are God…' <u>Then the fire of the Lord fell and consumed the burnt sacrifice</u> and the wood and the stones and the dust, and also licked up the water that was in the trench. When all the people saw it, they fell on their faces and they said, 'The Lord (Jehovah), He is God! The Lord, He is God'" (I Kings 19:22-39, *Emphasis mine*).

Prior to all the above referenced events, Elijah had challenged the backslidden, idol worshiping Israelites with these words: "How long will you halt and limp between two opinions? If the Lord (Jehovah) is God, follow Him! But if Baal, then follow him. And the people did not answer him a word" (I Kings 18:21, NKJV).

Again, what is our point? Our point is that the God of the Christians and Jews is a God of proofs and evidences as recorded in His holy book, the Bible. In addition to the proofs and evidences, we have already set forth that bear witness to the authenticity of Jehovah and His Book, let us view two Bible passages – one from the Old Testament and one from the New Testament. The prophet Isaiah records the following words of Jehovah:

> "For I am God, and there is no other;
> I am God, and there is none like me,
> Declaring the end from the beginning,
> And from ancient times things that are not yet done,
> Saying, My counsel shall stand,

And I will do all my pleasure" (Isa. 46:9-10).

This passage undoubtedly refers to <u>predictive prophecy which has been fulfilled</u>. We repeat, <u>prophecy</u> and <u>fulfillment</u> are <u>the unique purview</u> of the <u>Judeo/Christian faith</u>! <u>It is absent in other major religions.</u>

Now let's look at the New Testament witness of proof, texts that bear witness to the authenticity of Jehovah and the Bible. In the Book of Acts, the writer, Dr. Luke, spoke thusly of Jesus Christ and His resurrection: "He also presented Himself alive after His suffering by <u>many infallible proofs</u>, being seen by them during forty days and speaking of the things pertaining to the kingdom of God" (Acts 1:3, *Emphasis mine*).

The Apostle Paul offers <u>further eyewitness proof</u> of the resurrected Christ: "For I delivered to you first of all that which I also <u>received</u> (by direct revelation from the resurrected Christ who appeared in person to Paul); that Christ died for our sins <u>according to the Scriptures</u>, and that He was buried, and that He rose again the third day according to the Scriptures,

"And that He was seen by Cephas (Peter), then by the twelve, after that He was seen by <u>over five hundred brethren at once</u>...after that He was seen by James, then by all the Apostles, then last of all He was seen by me also..." (1 Cor.15:3-8, *Emphasis mine*).

In the passages above, the Apostle Paul gives clear, accurate and factual information about the <u>personal testimonies</u> of the <u>apostolic eyewitnesses</u> who saw the Risen Lord with their own eyes; and there were five hundred who saw Him at the <u>same time</u>. It is highly unlikely <u>that five hundred sound minded people</u> would have <u>seen the same thing</u> and <u>they all be mistaken</u>!

This is New Testament proof of the validity of the holy Bible's testimony. There is no such proof or evidence presented in the Quran or any other religious writings.

Clearly we have devoted a lot of space to the presenting of the validity and the authenticity of Jehovah God, the God, of the Jews and Christians, whose Holy Book, the Bible, is both <u>the divinely inspired word of the Living God</u>, and <u>it contains sound evidentiary proof</u> that it is <u>the truth</u> about the people, the Israelis, to whom Jehovah God gave the land known as the "Holy Land." Deadly wars have been and are being fought over this land. We have presented sound biblical evidence that Jehovah gave this land to Abraham, Isaac, Jacob and their descendants.

Chapter 4

Historical Realities

Muslims claim in the Quran that Allah gave <u>them</u> the Holy Land, and that Abraham sought to sacrifice Ishmael on mount Moriah, <u>instead of Isaac</u>, as recorded in the holy Bible in Genesis chapter twenty two (around 2,000 B.C.).

Allow me to wax anecdotal at this point. In 1985, my wife and I made our third tour of the Holy Land. At one point we were on the Mount of Olives. From that vantage point we could see the ruins of the Jewish temple which was destroyed in 70 AD. We could also see the hill called, "Golgotha." Our guide was in the process of explaining that <u>three</u> very important <u>biblical events</u> had occurred on the top of this mountain. As he explained, those three events were (1) the attempted offering of <u>Isaac</u> by Abraham as a burnt offering, (2) The building of the Jewish temple(s) and (3) the offering of the Lamb of God, our Lord Jesus Christ as a sacrifice for the sins of the whole world. Scarcely had the guide gotten into his discourse when someone standing behind me muttered, "It was Ishmael who was offered by Abraham on that mountain, not Isaac!" I turned and asked him (our bus driver, Hashim), "What did you say?" He repeated his first <u>unbiblical</u> assertion. I proceeded to ask him if he could read and pointed to the passage in Genesis chapter twenty two that clearly spoke of <u>Isaac</u>, Abraham's <u>second son</u> (whom God calls his "<u>only son</u>" in that chapter) as the one whom Abraham assayed to sacrifice. At that point Hashim became very agitated and drew a knife to strike me. Thank God, I moved out of harm's way! I learned only recently that that lie about Ishmael being the one Abraham attempted to offer is written in the Quran. Remember, the Old Testament was written some 2,500 years before the Quran was invented!

Let's look at a little religious history. Abraham fathered both Ishmael and Isaac around 2000 B.C. With the institution of the sign of circumcision (Gen. 17:10-13) Jehovah <u>birthed</u> the <u>Hebrew faith</u> through Abraham. When Isaac was weaned, Sarah his mother, insisted that Abraham cast Hagar the bond woman and her son Ishmael out of the family so that Ishmael might go to another land and beget a nation of his own. So, "He (Ishmael) dwelt in the Wilderness of Paran; and his mother <u>took</u> a <u>wife</u> for him <u>from</u> the land of <u>Egypt</u>" (Gen. 21:8-20). The people known as <u>Arabs</u> are in fact the nation that Ishmael begat, according to the Holy Bible. The Bible gives a prophetic description of Ishmael before he was born. The Angel of the Lord (a theophany of Jesus) appeared to Hagar as she fled from Sarai her mistress, and spoke these prophetic words to her:

> "Behold, you are with child,
> And you shall bear a son.
> You shall call his name Ishmael,
> Because the <u>Lord has heard</u> your affliction.
> "He <u>shall be a wild man</u>;
> His <u>hand shall be against every man</u>,
> And <u>every man's hand against him</u> and he
> Shall dwell in the presence of his brethren."
> (Gen. 16:11-12, *Emphasis mine*)

It is at this juncture that I would like to cite some interesting historical insights. <u>Judaism</u> was founded around <u>2000 B.C.</u> Christianity was founded around <u>33 A.D.</u> (the first century A.D.). Islam was founded by an <u>Arabian visionary</u>, a descendant of Ishmael, around <u>600 A.D.</u> (the 7th century A.D.). Obviously, Judaism was founded some 2000 years before Christianity and some 2500 years before Islam. Yet Islam, "the new kid on the block," has had the audacity of claiming that the

Judeo/Christian Scriptures were "corrupted" and it declares that both of these two older faiths are "false," because "The Quran teaches the true religion with God is Islam." The Quran emphasized of Allah, "There is no God but he, the Living. The everlasting." (A. S. Arberry, the Qur'an as Interpreted).

Muslims (Muhammedans) classify Jews and Christians as <u>unbelievers</u> or "<u>infidels</u>" – the latter because of our belief in the Holy Trinity. This youngest religion of the three major monotheistic religions, Islam, apparently sought to nullify the older two, calling them (Jews and Christians) <u>infidels</u>! The latter evidently set itself forth as being "wiser," more astute and superior in spiritual understanding to the two older and more established religious faiths. Upon close examination one can quickly perceive that Islam <u>borrowed</u> from Judaism and Christianity and <u>co-opted</u> the Old and New Testaments as products of Allah. Again, when one examines the Old and New Testaments of the Holy Bible and compares them to the Quran, one will quickly note their inner cohesiveness and superior quality of thought, order and inspiration that is grossly lacking and absent in the Quran.

Do you remember a few paragraphs back, we presented the <u>biblical beginning of the Arab nations</u> resulting from the co-habitation between Abraham and Hagar? Is there any wonder that Ishmael is the father of the people of Arabia? Remember the biblical prophecy that the Angel of Jehovah gave Hagar, Ishmael's mother, after she and the child were expelled from Abraham's household? The Angel Jehovah foretold that Ishmael would father his own great nation of twelve princes and a great multitude (Gen. 16:10, 17:20, and 21:18). Again, the Angel of Jehovah prophesied of the son, whom Abram named Ishmael: "<u>He shall be a wild man; his hand shall be against every man</u>" (Gen. 16:1-12). What are we saying? We are saying that the biblical prophecy concerning Ishmael, declared before his birth has its <u>fulfillment</u> in the <u>Arabian religion</u> (founded there) called <u>Islam</u>! Muhammed, (a descendant of Ishmael) founded his new religion on "supernatural visions and revelations" <u>he claimed</u> to have received through the angel Gabriel (Jehovah's messenger angel in both the Old and New Testaments) beginning in 610 A. D.

This new monotheistic religion came out of the "womb" fighting against every other religion declaring: "There is no God but Allah and Muhammed is his prophet!" In their fighting, antagonistic spirit (the spirit of Ishmael described in the Bible) they declared all other religious views to be false and their adherents to be "infidels." Islam was at its outset "spread by the sword." That's the way I heard Islam defined as a boy growing up. The word "Islam" means submission, and all who would not submit to the authority of Allah were to be killed by beheading.

This religion of Allah spread from Arabia throughout the Arabian Peninsula to Africa, the Middle East to Asia (Indonesia is the largest Muslim nation in the world) into Eastern Europe, and also into Spain in Western Europe.

"In less than a hundred years after the death of Muhammed, Islam had spread like wildfire over much of the known world" (The World Religions, Readers Digest, p. 93). By 1453 A.D. the Byzantine capital of Constantinople, capital of the "Holy Roman Empire" fell to the Ottoman Turks and became the capital of the "Muslim empire" known as the Ottoman Empire. Between 1517 and 1923 (around 400 years) Islam – personified by the Ottoman Caliphate (Territorial ruler) – spread from its base in Turkey across three continents. The French king, Charles Martel, defeated the Muslims at Poitiers in southern France in 732 (100 years after Muhammed's death) halting their expansion in the west (ibid, p. 93). Thus the rest of Western Europe was spared the sword of Islam in that

Historical Realities

day and time. Today Islam is spreading throughout Western Europe and the United States by means of <u>immigration</u> and <u>multiplication</u>.

For Muslims, the Quran is "the completion" of God's message to humankind and "the culmination" of all. When Muhammed received his "divine" call in a cave in 610 A.D., it is said that the majestic being, "Gabriel" of whom he is said to have had a vision told him to recite: "In the name of the Lord who created, man of a blood clot" (Quran 96:1-3). Jesus Christ the risen Lord calls Himself "The Alpha and the Omega, The Almighty" (Rev. 1:8). A tradition in Islam says, he, Mohammed was a prophet when Adam was still between water and clay. Then he was born in his created form <u>as the seal of the prophets</u>. (The last and greatest of the prophets – including Jesus the Messiah).

Jesus stated in the Parable of the wicked vinedressers, Matthew 21:36-37, "Again he (God the Father) sent other servants (prophets), more than the first, and they did likewise to them; then <u>last of all</u> he sent <u>his son</u> to them saying, they will respect my son!"

Jesus refers to <u>himself</u> here as the <u>last of the prophets</u> some 600 years before Muhammed was born! Therefore,

Jesus, out of His own mouth declares <u>Himself</u> to be the <u>last</u> or the <u>seal</u> of the prophets!" That makes Muhammed a liar!

Chapter 5

Muslims Resent Those Who Help Israel

Why do Muslims, even moderate Muslims, view the West with suspicion, distrust and sometimes even hatred? They hold a resentment toward the success of the West (so said Osama Bin Ladin and other architects of the 911 attack on America) and they have a desire for the glory of the Islamic past – a return to a unified Islamic empire. Islam traditionally places the world into two basic divisions – "The land of Islam (dar al-Islam)," and "the land of the unbeliever (infidel), or heretic (dar al-harb)," the latter eventually destined for <u>absorption</u> or <u>conquest</u> by Islam. One of Islam's <u>chief goals</u> is to <u>dominate</u> and <u>rule</u> the world! They purpose to impose Islamic, <u>Shari'a law</u> in every nation of the world. Their law controls the social, economic, political and religious aspects of their subjects' lives including the imposition of 7th century dress codes on women! As Ishmael claimed supremacy over his younger brother, Isaac, that is, relative to his being "bumped" out of his <u>firstborn position</u> and <u>rights</u>

in Abraham's family, one can clearly see Islam's superior attitude over Judaism and Christianity in exalting Muhammed over Jesus Christ and their Quran and other writings over the Holy Bible.

Islam's attitude of a "right to first place" can be seen in the height of their minarets (spires) on their mosques. They must always tower over every other building in town! It was not by mistake that the Dome of the Rock in Jerusalem, built in 691 A.D. (just 29 years after Mohammed's death) was built on top of the ruins of the Jewish (Herod's) temple in Jerusalem. That temple was destroyed and burned by Titus, the Roman general in 70A.D. The invasion and destruction of the Jewish temple was the result of many years of warnings by Jehovah's prophets to His people Israel to cease from their ungodly ways of disobedience and idolatry.

Israel rejected God's warnings and even rejected Jesus Christ, God's Son and the Jewish Messiah. They participated in His crucifixion and thus invited God's judgments upon themselves, their land and their temple.

Chapter 6

Israel's Claims Documented

Let's get back to the Holy Land and the claims of ownership of the land. As we pointed out in earlier chapters of this book, Jehovah God gave this disputed land to Abraham and his seed through Isaac and Jacob, by way of an <u>Everlasting Covenant</u> that Jehovah cut with Abraham (Gen. 15:7-21; 17:7-8;; 21:8-12; 25:5; 26:2-5; 28:1-4; 28:10-15; 35:9-13 and Josh. 1:1-6). Thus we have twelve different Bible references in different books that Jehovah gave this disputed land to Abraham's seed through Isaac and Jacob. Indeed there are many more Bible references to the above mentioned fact. It takes only <u>three</u> witnesses to establish a thing as being true in the Holy Bible (2 Corinthians 13:1).

Besides all these Scriptural references, we have the records of God's supernatural opening of the Red Sea. God's people crossed over it on dry ground in route to the Promised Land. We also have the record of the dividing of the River Jordan for God's people to cross over into the Land of Promise.

Biblical, historical records tell us that Joshua and the people of Israel invaded and possessed the Promise Land, "the land of Canaan," around <u>1400 to 1375 BC</u>, some 700 years after God covenanted with Abraham to give the land to Abraham's seed. Israel occupied that land, along with Canaanites (An Arab remnant), until <u>721 B.C. – some 700 years later</u>! At that time the Assyrian army attacked Israel's northern kingdom (the ten tribes) and carried them beyond the Black Sea due to Israel's persistent practice of idolatry and her persistent refusal to heed God's warnings through his prophets.

This was Israel's <u>first scattering and expulsion out of the Land</u> of Promise as the Lord had warned and foretold through Moses (Deut. 4:15-31). But the Lord also said, "When you are in distress and all these things (scattering, etc.) come upon you <u>in the latter days, when you turn to the Lord your God</u> and <u>obey His voice</u> (for the Lord your God is a merciful God), <u>He will not forsake you nor destroy you, nor forget the covenant of your fathers</u> which He swore to them" (Deut. 4:30-31). The ten tribes of Israel which were scattered among the nations by the Assyrians in 721 B.C., remain somewhat scattered until today, but Jehovah knows where every Israeli is!

In 597-582 B.C., Jerusalem fell to Nebuchadnezzar king of Babylon. The prophet Jeremiah who remained in Jerusalem after the Judean captives were carried away to Babylon, penned a letter to the captives saying, "For thus says the Lord, 'After seventy years are completed at Babylon, I will visit you and perform My good word toward you, and cause you to return to this place (Jerusalem) (Jeremiah 29:10).'" Whereas Israel's ten tribes, the northern kingdom, remains scattered among the nations, Judah (some of them) the southern kingdom did indeed return to the Promised Land to Jerusalem, as the Prophet Jeremiah had said, after seventy years.

We pick up the story of Judah's return to Jerusalem as prophesied by Jeremiah in the book of the Ezra (around 538 B.C.),

"Now in the first year of Cyrus king of Persia, that the word of the Lord by the mouth of Jeremiah might be fulfilled, the Lord stirred up the spirit of Cyrus king of Persia so that he made a proclamation throughout all his kingdom, and also put it in writing, saying…, (Thus says Cyrus king of Persia: (All the kingdoms of the earth The

Lord God of heaven (Jehovah) has given me, and He has commanded me to build Him a house at Jerusalem which is in Judah (A far cry from what Ahmadinejad of Iran (Persia) would say today!) *(Emphasis added).* Who is among you of all His people? May his God be with him, and let him go up into Jerusalem which is in Judah and build the house of the Lord God of Israel (He is God), which is in Jerusalem..."' (Ezra 1:1-3).

Here we have another example of <u>predictive prophecy being fulfilled</u> as we cited previously. The Jews <u>did indeed return to Judah and Jerusalem</u> as the Lord spoke by the mouth of the prophet Jeremiah some 70 years before. By this time Babylon had fallen under the hand of the Persians.

I would be remiss if I failed to point out at this juncture that this same Cyrus, king of Persia, was identified some 200 years before he was born, by the prophet Isaiah. He was called by name. Let us listen in on Isaiah's prophecy from Jehovah to Cyrus:

"Thus says the Lord to His anointed, to Cyrus, whose right hand I have held, to subdue nations before him...I will go before you and make the crooked places straight...that you may know that <u>I, the Lord called you</u>

<u>by your name am the God of Israel…I have named you, though you have not known me</u>.

> "I am the Lord, and there is no other.
> There is no other God besides me.
> I will gird you, though you have not known me,
> "That they (the nations) may know from the rising of the Sun to its setting,
> That <u>there is none besides me</u>.
> "<u>I am the Lord, there is none other;</u>
> I form the light and create darkness,
> I make peace and create calamity;
> I, the Lord, do all those things"
> (Isa. 45:1-7, *Emphasis mine*)

So <u>the Jews did return</u> to <u>the land that Jehovah</u> had <u>given to their fathers</u> through Abraham, Isaac and Jacob around 2,000 B.C. On this occasion the seed of Jacob was out of the Promised Land for 70 years, returning around <u>459 B.C</u>.

Canaanites occupied their native land until most of them were conquered by or driven out by Joshua during his conquest of the land. Joshua did not drive all the Canaanites out of

Canaan, neither did he destroy them all as God commanded. Some of them continued to dwell in the land alongside the Israelites even until today. Surely at least some of them remained in the land. It is believed that the Edomites (the Esauites) and other Canaanite/Arab groups <u>never left</u> the land of Israel (please read Judges Chapters 1-5). Ironically the Holy Land was <u>derisively</u> called "<u>Palestine</u>" by the Roman conquerors when they invaded Israel, slaughtered millions, and drove the rest of them out during their invasion in 70 A.D. The name <u>Palestine</u> was derived from the <u>Philistines</u>, Israel's ancient enemy.

When the Israelites were carried out of the Holy Land by the Assyrians in 721 B.C., later, in 70 A.D., when the remaining Jews were driven out of the land by Titus the Roman general, they wound up by and large in Europe. Some Jewish diaspora have been found in China, India, Africa and other remote places. They were truly <u>scattered throughout the world</u>. While a few Jews and Arab Bedouins (nomadic herdsmen) remained in the Holy Land throughout history, the vast majority of Jews could be found in Russia, Poland (and other parts of Eastern Europe), England, Italy and other European countries.

The dispersed Jews often suffered harsh persecution and isolation in many European countries. Germany and Poland became the worst of the Jewish persecutors which culminated in the Holocaust in which 6 million Jews were brutally slaughtered by the Germans. This slaughter took place between the late 1930's through the mid 1940's when Germany (Hitler) was defeated by the American Allied Forces!

The "Back to Zion" Movement began in 1897 in Switzerland. It was led by an Austrian Jewish journalist named, Theodore Herzl. He died in 1904, but his movement continued to grow. "Then, on November 2, 1917 the British government...issued its momentous Balfour Declaration, expressing the British government's support for the 'establishment in Palestine of a national home for the Jewish People.' And in, 1919, the U.S. President, Woodrow Wilson, confirmed the Balfour Declaration in a letter to the leading German-American Rabbi, Stephen Wise" (THE WORLD'S RELIGIONS Readers Digest Page 36).

Having mentioned earlier that Jehovah had warned His people Israel that their disobedience, idolatry and backslidings which would lead to their expulsion from the Holy Land, the Lord also made some powerful promises about their return to and reinstatement into the Holy Land.

The prophet Isaiah wrote the following:

"It shall come to pass in that day (after Christ's first coming) that The Lord shall set His hand again the second time. "To recover the remnant of His people who are left...He will set up a banner for the nations, "And will assemble the outcast of Israel, and gather together the dispersed of Judah from the four corners of the earth" (Isa. 11:11-12, *Emphasis mine*).

Again, the prophet Ezekiel spoke the word of the Lord saying:

"Surely I have spoken in my burning jealousy against the rest of the nations and against Edom (Palestinians) who gave my land to themselves as a possession, with wholehearted joy and spiteful minds, in order to plunder its open country..."Therefore thus says the Lord God, 'I have raised my hand in an oath that surely the nations that are around you, shall bear their own shame. But you O mountains of Israel, you shall shoot forth your branches and yield your fruit to my people Israel, for they

<u>are about to come</u> (and they have come since April 14, 1948!)...I will make you (The Holy Land) <u>inhabited as in former times</u>, and do better for you than at your beginnings. Then you shall know I am the Lord. 'Yes, I will cause men to walk on you, My people Israel; They shall take possession of you, and you shall be their inheritance; no more shall you bereave them of children'...'Son of man, <u>when the house of Israel dwelt in their own land, they defiled it by their own ways and deeds</u>...'Therefore <u>I poured out my fury on them....for their idols</u> with which they had defiled it. So I <u>scattered them among the nations,</u> and they were dispersed throughout the countries...When they came to the nations wherever they went, they profaned my holy name-when they (their captors) said of them, these are <u>the people of the Lord,</u> and <u>yet they have gone out of His land</u>...And I will sanctify my great name, which has been profaned among the nations, which you have profaned in their midst; and the nations shall know I am the Lord...For <u>I will take you from among the nations,</u> <u>gather you out of all countries,</u> and <u>bring you into your own land</u> (Israel)...<u>Then you shall dwell in the land</u> that I gave your fathers: (Abraham, Isaac and Jacob) you shall be my people and I will be your God'" (Ezek, 36:5-12, 17-28, *Emphasis mine*).

Please take note that Isaiah lived and prophesied for the Lord in the 8th century B.C. Ezekiel lived and prophesied in the 6th century B.C. These two prophets foretold Israel's return to the land Jehovah gave to Abraham, Isaac and Jacob many centuries before Israel returned to and resettled in that land in the 20th century A.D.-May 14, 1948.

The return of the tribes of Israel to the Holy Land and their gathering and resettling there is a divine feat of awesome propositions! If the exodus of Israel out of Egypt through the miraculously opened Red Sea was momentous, then their preservation as a people and religious community is nothing less than miraculous! The Israelites survived 2,500 years of severe persecutions, slavery and several attempts at their extermination.

The Lord confirmed the predictive prophecies of His holy prophets that spanned hundreds of years, by faithfully re-gathering his people, the Israelites and the Jews from the four corners of the earth. He restored them back into the land that He swore by an Everlasting Covenant to their fathers, Abraham, Isaac and Jacob. The prophetic or any other kind of evidence to support the Arabs' (Ishmael's seed or the Palestinian's) claim to the Holy Land is sparse and weak at best. <u>Israel's claims</u> to the Land <u>are legal, copious and in great abundance!</u>

There are some references in the Quran citing Ishmael as Abraham's rightful heir to the Holy Land. However, <u>Islam came into being some 2,500 years after Israel</u> was well established under Abraham! The <u>dye had been well cast</u> by the time Islam came along, that the <u>Holy Land was the sole possession of the Jewish and Israeli people</u> by Jehovah's decree and <u>Everlasting Covenant.</u> The Arab Muslim people felt since their inception that the Arab people, the offspring of Ishmael, were defrauded by Jehovah who gave Ishmael's birthright (<u>first born</u> of Abraham) to Isaac the younger half-brother instead.

Chapter 7

Insights into Islam's Deceptive Claims on the Holy Land

The book "FAST FACTS ON ISLAM," poses a question on pages 134-135 which is: "What do Palestinian Religious Authorities Teach? Palestinian spiritual leaders, all appointed by the Palestinian Authority (PA) political leadership have consistently and openly <u>taught that the current conflict between Palestinian Arabs and the Israeli Jews is part of an eternal religious war between Islam and the Jewish people.</u> Sermons and religious instruction that are broadcast every Friday on official Palestinian TV and radio, as well as religious lessons that appear in PS newspapers and other media, show this un-mistakenly. <u>Jewish people are portrayed as the permanent enemies of Allah, and the destruction of Jews is represented to be the will of Allah.</u> 'On the national level, Allah prohibits acceptance of Israel's existence and will destroy it...'"

Other positions of the Palestinian Authority concerning the Holy Land can be found in the following statements:

>1. All land between the Mediterranean Sea and the Jordan River (that is, all of Israel) is an Islamic religious trust (a wage). Indeed any Muslim who surrenders any part of this land to Israel is fated to Hell.
>2. Any accord with Israel is intrinsically impermanent, signed merely because of Israel's temporary military advantage.
>3. Allah will discipline Muslim believers who evade their responsibility to war against Israel.
>4. "The ultimate annihilation of Israel is assured by Allah." (FAST FACTS ON ISLAM page 135).

Let's listen in on a Palestinian Authority Broadcast:

"...Their Bible (of the Jews) today, has no light and no teachings. Their Bible today, is just a bunch of notes that were written down by people who lie about God, his prophets and his Bible.

"Those who do these kinds of things are descendants of Abelis, meaning the descendants of the satans.

"They fabricated a Jewish history book full of promises to Abraham, Isaac and Jacob that He will give them the land of Palestine..."

(Religion class on Palestinian Television, 3 November, 1998) (FAST FACTS ON ISLAM, page 137)

Here's more of the same:

"All of the agreements entered (with Israel) are temporary, until the decree comes from Allah and until the destiny from Allah is realized" (Dr. Muhammed Ibrahim Madi, Palestinan Television, 28 July 2000) (FAST FACTS OF ISLAM, page 137).

Thus we see today the extreme ends to which Arabs will go to denounce and deny Israel's legitimate claim to the Holy Land. They resort to the worst kind of exaggeration, lies and invective to justify their "right" to the Holy Land.

From a purely human standpoint, the anger of the Arabs against their cousins, the Jews, seems somewhat justified. According to their culture and history, Isaac, Abraham's younger son, "defrauded" Ishmael, Abraham's firstborn son (and Ishmael's half-brother) out of his birthright, which included the Holy Land. The world at large, including the United Nations, is <u>against</u> Israel and <u>for</u> the Palestinians. They erroneously charge Israel with aggression against Palestine, whereas, true history reveals that Israel has been attacked time and again by united Arab armies. Israel has beaten back the Arab hordes and defeated them every time. That's because <u>the God of heaven and earth is on Israel's side</u> and has fought for them! Is it not time that the world wake up and smell the coffee? I recently heard a Roman Catholic bishop on the "60 Minutes" TV program denounce Israel's right to call Palestine their "Promised Land." He claimed there is no sacred Scripture to support that claim. <u>I beg to differ!</u>

Let's view a bit more of the Holy Land history.

"The Palestinians of today are not descended from the Philistines of the Bible and never lived as a sovereign ruled nation. Until the inception of Modern Israel, they dwelt as scattered nomadic family tribes, alongside Jewish neighbors, on whose lands whose boundaries were not drawn into states until after World War I. During the centuries Jews and Arabs sometimes coexisted peaceably, but violence and terror often erupted at the call of Muslim leaders driven by jihad and/or pure hate.

"In 1920, the League of Nations (predecessor to the UN) handed Great Britain a mandate to secure the establishment of a Jewish home in Palestine. The territory reserved for the Jews encompassed not only all of present-day Israel, <u>but also all of what is today known as Jordan.</u> The mandate was scarcely issued when Arab rioting began in order to protest the future existence of a Jewish state...Terror was not conceived by frustrations of life in refugee camps; that tactic is at least as old as Islam.

"Ironically, the vast majority of the Arabs denying the creation of Israel had immigrated to Palestine from surrounding areas <u>only after</u> the Zionist pioneers began to reclaim the land in the early twentieth century. With the Jews came new job opportunities and improved medical care...Later, countless others poured in from neighboring countries – not to carry on normal lives, but to undermine establishing the Zionist state...Wielding terror and oil as tools of intimidation, the Arabs persuaded Britain in 1922 to grant them a full 78 percent of the land allotted to the Jews...Predictably Arab rioting and terror persisted until Britain finally turned the political foray over to the newly created UN. Continuing the policy of Arab appeasement, the UN sliced off 22 percent of the original mandate for a Jewish homeland into two states: One Jewish and one Palestinian Arab. The Partition Plan of 1947 recognized the

Jews right to sovereign control over a sliver of space amounting to <u>a mere 10 percent of the world community's original Mandate.</u> The same plan offered the Arabs who lived within Mandate territory another Palestinian State in addition to Jordan, consisting of Judea, Samaria and Gaza.

"The Jews accepted the plan: the Arabs rejected it…they (the Arabs) wanted it all – a pan-Arab Islamic empire spanning the entire Middle East leaving no place on earth for a Jewish nation…" (WHY CARE ABOUT ISRAEL? By Sandra Teplinsky, pp. 190-192, *Emphasis mine*).

"On May 14, 1948, at exactly 4:00 P.M., Israel's first Prime Minister, David Ben-Gurion delivered Israel's Declaration of Independence. Ben-Gurion made the following statement during his Declaration of Independence speech (concerning the Rebirth of Israel):

'By virtue of the natural and historic right of the Jewish people…we hereby proclaim the establishment of the Jewish state in Palestine, <u>to be called the State of Israel</u>…for the fulfillment of the dream of generations – <u>the redemption of Israel</u>" (ibid, p.192, *Emphasis mine*).

"The survival of the Jewish nation proved nothing short of miraculous. Aided by the armies of heaven, Israel defended her borders and held her ground. But by the time a cease-fire went into effect, those areas the UN had allocated for a separate Arab Palestinian state were illegally annexed and occupied – not by Israel, but by Jordan and Egypt. Now, the Arabs' publicly stated goal in the war had been to liberate Palestine. But neither Jordan nor Egypt ever gave the territories (Judea, Samaria and Gaza) they 'liberated' back to the Palestinians. Why not? The reason is that the pan-Arab plan, had they won the war, was to divide up Israel among themselves, leaving nothing for sovereign Palestine, let alone Jewish rule…"

"…The aftermath of Israel's fight for independence (a war she did not start) left large numbers of refugees in the Middle East…Arab hatred of Israel perpetuates Palestinian privation. That the world faults Israel – and would threaten her survival – for an Arab-generated Arab problem is another instance of a big lie, repeated long enough." (ibid p. 193-194, *Emphasis mine*).

"What are the real roots of this (Arab/Palestinian-Israeli) Conflict? (The very question our book title raises)…That Palestinians want a homeland and Muslims want control over sites they consider holy? These two demands are nothing more than strategic deceptions, propaganda ploys. They are nothing more than phony excuses and rationalizations for the terrorism and murdering of Jews. <u>The real goal of those making these demands is the destruction of the state of Israel</u>" (WHY CARE ABOUT ISRAEL? cited Joseph Rarah, World Net Daily (www.worldnetdaily.com), as cited in <u>Jewish Voice Today</u>, no. 3, (July-August 2002:11, *Emphasis mine*).

Once again, we say that we have demonstrated from a sound handling of the written word of God (the Holy Bible) that the Holy Land was and is indeed <u>Jehovah's gift</u> to Abraham, Isaac and Jacob – by <u>His own sovereign choice!</u> The Palestinians and Muslims do not have a valid claim to the ownership of the Holy Land! Israel suffers under the cloud of negative public opinion and the UN's negative attitude against Israel.

"In the Arab world there is a false peacemaking concept based on a precedent set by Mohammed in dealing with his enemies of the Qurayish tribe. The Hudaitbiya agreement established the right within Islam, called <u>Hudna</u>, to fake peace when you are weak so you can wait for better timing to conquer your enemy.

"While the Oslo Accords were ongoing, Arafat admitted, 'I do not consider the (Oslo) agreement any more than the agreement which was signed by our prophet Mohammed and the Qurayish! 'Former Israeli Prime Minister Ehud Barak, said the following at the Camp David meeting:

'What they want is a Palestinian State in all of (Israel)...They are products of a culture in which to tell a lie...creates no dissonance. They don't suffer from the problem if telling lies that exist is the Judeo-Christian culture. Truth is seen (by Muslims) as an irrelevant category. <u>There is only that which serves your purpose and that which doesn't</u>. They see themselves as emissaries of a national movement for which everything is permissible'" (WHY CARE about ISRAEL? p. 203, *Emphasis mine*).

Chapter 8

The Church and Others against the Jews

Why do some Christian leaders today deny that Israel has a <u>right</u> to possess the Holy Land? Well, first of all, we must take a look back into Christian theological history concerning the attitude of the church regarding Israel.

Under the heading of "Severing Jewish Roots" the author, Sandry Teplinsky ("Why Care about Israel?") says, "Many of our most influential, early church fathers rejected the spiritual roots that supported them (Israel). Instead of sharing in the 'nourishing sap' God intended, they turned away and tapped headlong into the deadly poison of anti-Semitism."

She goes on to say, "Paul's warning to Gentile believers about pride went unheeded (Rom. 11:18-21). The church had become overwhelmingly Gentile, so it reasoned that there was no more need for the support of the root (Israel). What presumption! ...Gentiles (*Emphasis mine*) claimed to have replaced Israel. Church fathers taught that the unfaithfulness of the Jewish people resulted in a collective guilt which made them subject to the permanent curse of God" (Marvin R. Wilson, "Our Father, Abraham: Jewish Roots of the Christian Faith").

"Emperor Constantine made Christianity the official religion of Rome in 312 A.D. In so doing, he married the church and the state, injecting 'theological' anti-Semitism throughout the polity...With Constantine's Christendom, the notion of portraying Jews as the killers of Jesus originated – never to vanish...

"At first glance Christian anti-Semitism would appear to be an oxymoron, something totally contradictory. Unfortunately, it is not. The seeds were sown early in Christian history...Replacement theology and/or super secessionism also had its beginnings in early Church history..."

In 1543, the beloved herald of the Protestant Reformation, Martin Luther, instructed his followers with these words:

"Whenever they (Jews) have their synagogues, nothing is found but a den of devils...What shall we Christians do with this rejected and condemned people, the Jews? ...First set fire to their synagogues or schools...I advise that their rabbis be forbidden to teach hence forth on pain of loss of life...I advise that safe conduct on the highway be abolished completely for the Jews. If this does not help, <u>we must drive them out like mad dogs</u> ("Martin Luther, The Jews and their Lies").

"Luther's words set a dark tone in Germany – one that, five hundred years later, Adolf Hitler exploited to unimaginable horrors...

"In rejecting Jewish roots, Christianity took aim at one segment of the Church in particular – Messianic Jews" (WHY CARE ABOUTH ISRAEL? pp 114-115).

Anti-Jewish sentiment within the church dates back as far as the first and second century church fathers.

The Liberal Churches in history are not the only Christians who have hated and currently hate Jews, there are others. Today many <u>Palestinian</u> Christians embrace the liberal church view of <u>Replacement Theology</u>. They downplay God's present restoration of Israel.

"They interpret the Scriptures symbolically or allegorically rather than literally, so that any right to the land the Jews may have once had is now superseded by the New Covenant Church." One noted Christian leader expressed the local (Palestinian) consensus on this wise:

"(The) concept of a promised land is expired to give way to the new concept of the kingdom of God, which resides in every believer's heart" (Ibid. p. 207).

Palestinian Jews take the position (from Replacement Theology) that the Bible does not justify the existence of the State of Israel. They along with the historic Christian church inflated with anti-Semitism could hope for Israel to not only not have a place in the Holy Land. Their preference is that Israel did not exist at all!

But God, says not so! As we have pointed out earlier in this book, the Lord spoke quite clearly through the prophets Isaiah and Ezekiel that He would <u>recover His scattered people Israel</u>, and <u>restore them back into their ancient Homeland</u> - in the <u>latter days</u>! The Lord did this on May 14, 1948, to the chagrin of many!

The Apostle Paul, the Hebrew Apostle to the Gentiles, (the non-Jews of the world) made the following awesome statement to the church at Rome:

"For if their (Israel's) being cast away is the reconciling of the world, what will their acceptance (restoration) be but life from the dead" (Rom.11:15)?

There you have it. The Creator God of the heavens and the earth, the One who gives life to all and even raises the dead, did just that. He raised Israel from the dead or from the seemingly non-existence – after some two thousand years! The truth is that God has kept His word!

Yes, I am certain and I am sure that the ancient descendants of Abraham, Isaac and Jacob have been, by God's stated will, restored to their ancient homeland in the Middle East. Allow me to use an anecdotal experience in this regard. When my wife, Deborah and I married in 1958, we stayed with her family for a few months thereafter. During that time my late mother-in-law used to listen to a Dr. Fuller on the radio quite often. That dear preacher would plead with his listening audience to accept <u>the truth</u> in the Bible that God was fulfilling Bible prophecy in resettling His people Israel into their ancient land. It was only after the Lord impressed my heart to write this book that the Holy Spirit brought that radio broadcast back to my remembrance. It was the Lord's way of bearing witness with my spirit that He had indeed moved upon me to write this book.

As we move toward our conclusion, allow me to reiterate that the basic <u>root</u> and <u>cause</u> of the age old conflict over the Holy Land, was a <u>family feud</u> in Abraham's family between his firstborn son Ishmael by his bondwoman, Hagar, and his younger son, Isaac, the son of promise by his wife Sarah. The hatred and anger of the Arab people against their cousins the Jews has grown deeper and stronger over the years. They still feel they were defrauded of their "rightful" ownership of the Holy Land (Palestine) because Ishmael was Abraham's <u>firstborn</u> son. Their anger over the years has been fueled by their religion, <u>Islam</u>, which from its inception fostered hatred of and promoted the killing of Jews.

I would be remiss if I failed to point out that <u>God loves the Arab people</u> even as He loves all the people of the world. The New Testament declares, "For <u>God so loved the world that He gave His only begotten Son, that whosoever believes in Him should not perish but shall have eternal life</u>" (John 3:16). <u>Ishmael</u>, the father of the Arab nations, <u>was so special to God</u> in the Bible, that the Angel of the Lord (Old Testament theophany or appearances of Jesus) appeared to his mother <u>twice</u> to assure her that he had <u>a special place in God's heart</u>.

We repeat, God the Father and Jesus Christ His Son, the <u>Savior of the world</u>, loves the Arabic people deeply! Today, Muslim/Arab countries like Saudi Arabia, Egypt and others <u>outlaw</u> the open preaching of the gospel of Jesus Christ. They call it <u>proselytizing</u>! If one is found preaching about Christ, salvation, etc., such a person could be imprisoned or even killed. If a Muslim in any of those countries confesses Jesus Christ as his Savior and Lord, he or she can legally be put to death.

Since that is the case, and Jesus loves the Arab Muslims very much, it is commonly reported that He is appearing to many of these spiritually hungry people in visions and dreams. What He reportedly says to these persons is,

"I am the way, the truth and the life, follow Me!" We are aware of reports of this happening quite often nowadays. Why is Jesus Christ doing things this way? Because He is superseding the walls built by devilish men to get His truth to those who desire to receive it. Ishmael was <u>circumcised</u> with all the males in Abraham's household

(Gen, 17:23-27), which means that he and his descendants will one day share in Jehovah's <u>spiritual</u> covenant blessings, even as some of them <u>now enjoy natural covenant blessings, such as oil!</u> (See Isaiah 19:23-24)

We have attempted to point out what "the Root and Causes of the Middle East Conflict" are. We know we have given you the major reasons for the conflict over the Holy Land, but we have not exhausted the subject. The prophet Ezekiel foretold an awesome war against Israel in their land involving a coalition of Gentile nations such as Russia, Iran, Sudan, Libya and others.

Chapter 9

Here's God's Remedy for the Age Old Conflict

The Lord Himself will draw those nations that will attack Israel and make war against her into His land to destroy them and to hallow His name that has been defiled also by the nations that took Israel into captivity. This war is described in Ezekiel chapters 38 and 39. The Lord concludes by saying, "Then they (Israel) shall know that <u>I am the Lord their God, who sent them into captivity among the nations, but also brought them back to their land</u>, and none of them are captive any longer. <u>And I will not hide my face from them anymore</u>; for I shall have poured out my Spirit on the <u>house of Israel</u>, says the Lord God" (Ezek. 39:28, *Emphasis mine*).

Satan, the chief enemy of God in this world, has one aim – "To steal, and to kill and to destroy" (the words of Jesus found in St. John 10:10b). Jesus further described the devil on this wise, "He was a murderer from the beginning, and he does not stand in the truth, because there is no truth in him…for he is a liar and the father of it" (St. John 8:44b).

The followers of Islam, especially in Palestine, are given to the ways of Satan in that they <u>speak deceit</u> about the Holy Land. With reference to the Camp David talks in the year 2,000, "The Palestinians – actually the whole Arab Muslim world engaged in holy war against Israel – cannot end the conflict with anything less than ending Israel" (WHY CARE about ISRAEL? p. 202).

<u>Palestinian Muslims are bent on killing Israelis and possessing the Holy Land at any cost!</u> Safa, a Muslim from birth and now an active Spirit filled, born again Christian evangelist, says the following about Islam and its nature:

"Islam has left a finger print of blood through every page of its history, beginning with <u>Hijra</u>, the onset of Islam, up to this very day."

"The spirit that advocated Islam is a blood-thirsty spirit which rages war and division. It is a spirit of revenge and retaliation. Its purpose is to create hate, sorrows, mourning and confusion."

Hussein Musawi, the leader of the Islamic Amal movement made the following statement:

"This path is the path of blood, the path of martyrdom. For us death is easier than smoking a cigarette, if it comes while fighting for the cause of God (Allah) while defending the oppressed."

The author, Safa, goes on to say:

"Where this spirit is permitted, there will be terror and fear. This spirit feeds on fear and death – <u>the very work and nature of Satan</u>. Though Muslim scholars try to justify the acts, teachings and laws of Islam, they cannot deny the history of bloodshed that Islam has left upon the pages of human history" (Inside Islam, pp. 36-37).

Let's return to our theme, "The Root, the Causes and the Remedy of the Middle East Conflict." We repeat, the root causes of the wars, tensions and disagreements over the Promised Land was a <u>family feud</u> in Abraham's house. Jehovah God Himself chose to change the "rules of the game" concerning the law of primogenitor – the law of the <u>double portion</u> of the inheritance going to the <u>firstborn son</u>. The Lord elected to assign <u>the inheritance</u>

and <u>the blessing</u> of Abraham (which included the Promised Land) to <u>Isaac the second born son</u>, instead of Ishmael, the firstborn son. When Ishmael and his mother Hagar were expelled from Abraham's household and family, the battle was on. Add to the mix Israel's idolatry and ultimate expulsion from the land, and the rise of Ishmael's volatile and violent religion, Islam, that occupied and laid claim (via the Quran,) to the land.

Then the Lord, by His own prophetic maneuverings and divine orchestrations, legally and officially restored Israel and replanted her back into His (their) land. <u>This is His remedy!</u>

As we conclude this book, let us look to three of the prophets of Israel to hear the conclusion of this matter. Before we go to the prophet Ezekiel per se, let's listen to Sandra Treplensky's analysis of his prophecy:

"God once gave the prophet Ezekiel a message to deliver to 'the mountains of Israel'; which He also called the 'ancient heights.' The message is in response to Israel's enemies seeking to overtake these high places. These mountains and ancient heights are located in Judea and Samaria – the <u>heartland of Israel – otherwise known as</u>

the West Bank or Palestine. Ezekiel's admonition applies astonishingly to the situation of our day.

"God denounces those staking claim to Judea and Samaria and terrorizing the country from every side. Then He chastises all other nations that have joined in the enemy's slander and occupation of the land" (WHY CARE about ISRAEL? p. 223).

The prophet Ezekiel declared, "Thus says the Lord God, 'Because the enemy has said of you, Aha! The ancient heights have become our possession.' Therefore prophesy and say, (Thus says the Lord God, "Because they made you (Israel) desolate and swallowed you up on every side, so that you became the possession of the rest of the nations and you are taken up by the lips of talkers (gossipers) *(emphasis mine)* and slandered by the people' – Therefore, O mountains of Israel hear the word of the Lord God! Thus says the Lord God to the mountains...and the cities that have been forsaken, which became plunder and mockery to the rest of the nations all around —

"Therefore, thus says the Lord God, 'surely I have spoken in my burning jealously against the rest of the nations and against all Edom (descendants of Esau and Arabic peoples (*emphasis mine*)…who gave my land to themselves as a possession (inheritance) (Ezekiel 6:2-5 NKJV, *Emphasis mine*).

The next prophetic witness of Jehovah we shall hear from is Joel. This Old Testament prophet of God declared the following words:

"For behold, in those days and at that time, (*emphasis mine*, in our day and time) when I bring back the captives of Judah and Jerusalem, I will gather all nations. And I will enter into judgment with them there on account of My people, My heritage Israel, whom they have scattered among the nations; they have divided up my land." (The United Nations divided the Promised Land between Syria, Jordan, the Palestinians, and the Israelis, *emphasis mine*).

Conclusion

Let us bring this book to its final conclusion. For this, let's turn to this little book of God's prophet, Obadiah.

"God's Judgment Day is near for all the godless nations. <u>As you have done (to Israel), it will be done to you. What you did will boomerang back and hit your own head.</u> Just as you probed on my holy mountain, all the godless nations will drink God's wrath. "They'll drink, drink and drink – they'll drink themselves to death. But not so on Mount Zion – there's respite there! A safe and holy place! "The family of <u>Jacob will take back their possessions from those who took them from them.</u> "That's when the family of Jacob will catch fire, the family of Joseph became fierce flame, <u>while the family of Esau will be straw.</u> Esau <u>will go up in flames</u>, nothing <u>left of Esau</u> but a <u>pile of ashes.</u>"

"People from the south will take over the Esau mountains (lands now held by Arab peoples; *emphasis mine*); people from the foothills will over run the Philistines."

"They'll take the forms of Ephraim and Samaria (the West Bank or Palestine) and Benjamin will take Gilead, earlier, Israelite exiles will come back and take Canaanite land to the north of Zarephath. "Jerusalem exiles from the far northwest in Sepharad will come back and take the cities in the south, "The remnant of the saved in Mount Zion will go into the Mountains of Esau "And rule justly and fairly, a rule that honors God's kingdom" (THE MESSAGE BIBLE, Obadiah 1:15-21, *Emphasis mine*).

May the Lord bless and anoint the eyes of the understanding of all who read the pages of this book. May you understand more fully "The Root, the Causes and the Remedy of the Middle East Conflict", that in the End, God's purposes are fulfilled!

About the Author

Dr. Aaron B. Claxton has been in Christ for over 50 years and has preached the gospel for more than 50 years. He has been married to his lovely wife, Deborah, for more than 50 years. They are the proud parents of six children (four boys and two girls), all have been called into the five-fold ministry. The Claxtons are also blessed with a host of grandchildren and great grandchildren.

Dr. Claxton's academic background includes earned degrees from Morgan State University, from the Mount Royal College of the Bible and from St. Mary's Seminary and University, where he pursued the academics for the Doctor of Ministry degree. He completed that degree in 1996 at the Family Bible Seminary. Dr. Claxton has been awarded two honorary Doctorate degrees from Christian International University. They are the Doctor of Divinity and the Doctor of Laws degrees. He received his PhD degree in Biblical Studies from Family Bible Seminary in May 2003.

In addition to this prolific masterpiece, Dr. Claxton has authored over 30 books of which 8 are published:

"God's Plan for the Sons of Ham – *a future and a hope*," "The Biblical View of the Rapture and the Second Coming," "Farrakhan, Islam and Jesus the Messiah," "The Blessings of the Lord is Upon the Tither," "First Fruits the Missing Offering," "Possessing Our Earthly Inheritance **Now!**" and "Caught Up to Meet Him."

Apostle Claxton, along with his wife, Deborah, founded and pastored the New Creation Christian Church in Baltimore, Maryland for twenty-three years. He has taught at three Bible Colleges and is well traveled, having preached the gospel across America and in sixteen nations around the world.

Dr. Claxton stands in the offices of Apostle and Bishop, formally overseeing one hundred plus churches in the U.S., and in East and West Africa and is presently being established in a global, apostolic ministry, along with his wife, Deborah in her apostolic ministry. He also sits on several International Ministry Boards. His oldest son, Apostle Aaron Bryan Claxton, along with his wife, Sheila, now pastor the headquarters church in Baltimore, which Dr. Claxton founded in 1968.

www.ingramcontent.com/pod-product-compliance
Lightning Source LLC
Chambersburg PA
CBHW050606300426
44112CB00013B/2091